Blackberry Whispers

To Nikki

may your whispers
never go unheard

Angela Ray

7-17-04

Blackberry Whispers

Angela Ray

A Mahogany Dime
Publication

Blackberry Whispers
By Angela Ray

Copyright © 2004 by Angela Ray

All rights reserved. No part of this book may be reproduced or transmitted in any form by any means, electronic or mechanical, including photocopying, recording or by information storage and retrieval system without written permission from the author.

Printed in the United States of America.

ISBN 0-9748823-0-5

"Circle of Sisters" painting by Eric McRay

Bookcover layout and design by MODINAT

A Mahogany Dime Publication
www.mahoganydime.com

*This book is dedicated to my parents,
Mitchell Leana and Curtis Ray.*

Acknowledgments

"To every thing there is a season, and a time to every purpose under heaven."
Ecclesiastes 3:1

I first acknowledge God, for through him all things are possible, even the realization that my season was not when I thought it was. To my parents, I thank you for your love, support, and encouragement. Even when you didn't understand my whispers, you never silenced my voice. To my sister Kimberly, thanks for hooking a sista up with funds when times were tight. No matter when I called, you always had my back. To my niece Kiara, I am so proud of you. You have already had your first poem published at the age of eight, which is a big accomplishment. You have prayed with me and encouraged me more than you will ever know. To my family, both the Rays and the Wiggins, thank you for blessing me with rich experiences, wisdom, and even discipline when I needed it.

To my book cover designer, logo designer, video production specialist, web site editor, MODINAT (http://home.earthlink.net/~modinat), words cannot express my gratitude for your faithfulness. You have gone above and beyond the duty of friendship. I know your multi-media company is about to blow up!

To Eric McRay (www.mcraystudios.com), I appreciate the use of "Circle of Sisters." Who knew that the picture Andrea, Sherida, Barbette, and I posed for would eventually make the cover of the book.

To my linesisters, chapter sisters, and all the distinguished sorors of Delta Sigma Theta Sorority, I am honored to be a part of you. In particular, Wande and Michelle, you both have kept me sane.

Thank you for the late night phone conversations, editorial input, collaborations, and advice throughout this process.

To all of my girls, Sabrina, Erica, Shema, Lashawnda, Joy, Joslyn, and the fellas, DeLon, Charles, Tim, Siddiq, John, Antuan (the president of my fan club), you all have been indeed a blessing to me.

A special thanks to my endorsers, William Fredrick Cooper, Queen Sheba (www.oyaxclusive.com), and Tee C. Royal (www.rawsistaz.com); you all make me want to buy the book from myself. I appreciate your time and words. And, to Dr. Bediako, your foreword is priceless. I hope that I can live up to your prophetic words.

To the very talented Suzanne Douglas, I have to recognize you. The conversation we had at the National Black Theatre Festival encouraged me to move forward with my poetry.

To everyone else; Making it Count crew, Phillip Shabazz and Spirithouse, fellow poets, church family, friends, associates, and supporters, please know that I am deeply grateful to have fellowshipped with you all. And, if I have missed anyone by name, please forgive me.

TABLE OF CONTENTS

Foreword

CHITCHAT

Nothing   2

Mama's Lap   4

A Mahogany Dime   6

Maids in Waiting   8

At the Cross   10

Death   12

Countdown   14

Cuz We Country   17

How it Used to Be   19

Mother May I   21

Not Fair   22

THE JUICE

My Country   26

A Dream I Had   27

Dead End on a One Way Street   30

Colors   32

Little Black Girl   34

Sticks and Stones   36

Waiting to Excel   38

A New Declaration   40

MELLOW MURMURS

Mirror Mirror   44

Red Light Special   46

Ghost   47

An Intimate Disclosure Session   49

Heavy Heart   51

Poetry   55

Sunset   56

Beating the Blues   57

Dark Star   60

Forbidden Fruit   62

Black History   64

The Black Family Prevails   65

LIGHT VIBES AND SPOKEN WORD

Prelude to a Kiss   68

A Fallen Hero   72

Playing Your Fool   75

Chestnut Brown   79

An Independent Black Woman's Rebuttal   81

Take Me Back   85

Foreword

Merriam Webster's Collegiate Dictionary defines *renaissance* as "a movement or period of vigorous artistic and intellectual activity; a rebirth, revival". To many of us, the word *renaissance* typically conjures images of the first mecca of the African American creative aesthetic – 1920's Harlem. We would imagine street orators standing on the corner of 125th Street and Lenox Avenue, speaking on any topic ranging from religion to Pan-Africanism. We could hear the latest sounds emanating from jazz clubs as we make our way up Striver's Row. We might even nonchalantly bump into Langston Hughes or Zora Neale Hurston on our way to catch the downtown "A" train. Life undoubtedly felt "new" and "electric" in those days.

Fast-forward approximately 80 years and take a journey about 8 hours south of the cultural epicenter we know as Harlem. Upon arrival, you will find a place that is the epicenter for another artistic renaissance of sorts: the Triangle area of North Carolina. In recent years, several singers, musicians, writers, thespians, and artists from Raleigh, Durham, and Chapel Hill have emerged on the national scene – often with rave reviews. The common denominator of this collective tribe is that they have found a voice to express the life values of our people and creatively paint portraits of our problems <u>and</u> our possibilities. In that artistic vanguard, one voice in particular has softly whispered its way into our hearts and minds – the voice of Angela Ray. In *Blackberry Whispers*, Angela's poetry speaks honestly to our souls. As a 21st century griot, she continues in the tradition of those who are able to integrate what Hubert Harrison, the great Harlem cultural critic and intellectual, referred to as the "understanding of the Head...[and] the warm intuitions of the Heart."

Ms. Ray's current literary effort represents a rebirth and revival of those who "take it back to the essence." That is, she astutely reflects on the past in order to articulate a means by which we can create a meaningful future. The vivid images she creates are inspiring to young and old, male and female, and even to both the bourgeoisie and the proletariat. Years from now, when we reflect on the meaning of this epoch in our cultural and creative history, I am certain that some will say that the *renaissance* started with a whisper. **A Blackberry Whisper.**

Shawn Moyo Bediako
Cincinnati, Ohio

Shawn M. Bediako

Shawn M. Bediako is a community activist, health psychologist, and creative artist who currently resides in Cincinnati. While focusing the majority of his energy on social issues related to manhood development and health promotion, Bediako also pursues his artistic interests.

In 2001, Bediako self-published *epiphenomena*, a volume of love poems that he began writing in 1994. As a songwriter, his work has appeared on a recent release by the Urban Underground record label based out of San Jose, California. Currently, he does freelance compositions and arrangements for a variety of artists and is finishing production on his own solo project, a spoken-word/hip hop album scheduled for release in 2005 on Emerge Records.

A graduate of the University of Central Arkansas, Bediako earned a master's degree in community psychology from Florida A & M University and a doctorate in social/health psychology from the State University of New York at Stony Brook. He is an assistant professor of psychology at the University of Cincinnati.

CHITCHAT

Nothing

An old lamp sits on the dresser
without a shade to perfect its light.
The crackle from the wood blocks
in the cast iron heater ignite like
fire crackers on the 4th of July.
Calm enters the room.

I sit alone glaring at the snow-filled frame
of the thirteen-inch black and white
supported by a floor model Curtis Mathis.
Another hopeful star's future is dimmed by the
dreaded earsplitting reverberation of the
famous gong. With nothing to do, my curiosity
of activities throughout the house prompts my sudden
exit from the room.

A diffused flicker faintly falls on the bed.
My perceptiveness painted a picture of naked bodies.
"What y'all doing?" I asked knowingly.
"Nothing", my aunt responded
as the movement ceased.

Nothing appeared to be something, and I was
going to do everything to uncover the mystery.

Seeking confirmation,
my hand embraced the lamp, briefly.
"Don't turn on that light!"
my aunt exclaimed
in a moment of desperation.

Intimidation ruled, and I simply departed
rather defeated.

Reflecting on what I had almost seen,
a delightful smirk danced across my lips.
Grandma would be home soon
and nothing could stop me from telling.

Mama's Lap

It's where life began
where life emerged
and where life continues.

I remember Saturday evenings
sitting on Mama's lap,
watching television
drinking Kool-aid
or the hot trickle of Sulfur 8
oozing down the back of my ear
as she pulled the straightening comb
through my virgin hair.

Sunday mornings at church
sitting on Mama's lap was tradition-
listening to the preacher
sipping the last drop of grape
juice from the communion cup,
or chewing a piece of a buttermilk biscuit
from breakfast.

Weekday afternoons, Mama's
lap was a comfort for my head
and tears when I'd
fallen off my swing set
or been pushed off the slide
by an older cousin.

When company came over,
I sat in deafening silence
as I listened to the women
trade recipe secrets,
discuss the soaps,

and laugh about old times.

No one can return to their mother's womb,
the safety net of maternal love.
But sitting on Mama's lap
always makes me feel at home.

A Mahogany Dime

A Mahogany Dime is a brilliant being.
The perfect ten of African descent: caramel, honey, dark brown
the mystic medleys of our tones, like precious jewels on a crown.
Intellectual, confident, strong, eloquent,
For every woman, she is the true paradigm.
The quintessential lady, a Mahogany Dime.

A Mahogany Dime is a spiritual sista.
She gives her tenth, knowing she's a ten.
She believes in God for He dwells within.
Steadfast, faithful, earnest, merciful,
The core of her soul is indeed sublime.
No doubt, she is a Mahogany Dime.

A Mahogany Dime is a wonderful wife.
She's devoted to her husband and is still a good mother.
Her house is in order for she's forsaken all others.
Nurturing, admirable, loving, adorable,
Her pledge to her family is for a lifetime.
Naturally, she is a Mahogany Dime.

A Mahogany Dime is a competent cook.
Soul food is born in her kitchen: fried chicken, collard greens,
gravy on homemade biscuits, served with yams & lima beans,
Delectable, enticing, tempting, tantalizing,
Like her succulent steaks, she is indeed prime.
Always appetizing, a Mahogany Dime.

A Mahogany Dime is a fit female.
Her work-out is diverse. She runs, lifts, and swims,
sometimes training at home when she can't get to the gym.
Muscular, athletic, vigorous, majestic,
She knows her temple also demands time.

That's why she's a Mahogany Dime.

A Mahogany Dime is a distinctive dame.
She is not perfect by nature, yet her essence is without flaw.
Her resplendent radiance induces any man's awe.
Sensual, rhythmic, sexy, Afrocentric,
Sharing her company is eternal summertime.
That's what makes her a Mahogany Dime.

Maid in Waiting

Gon' get me some education.
Degrees make you free.
A B. A. from A & T
Drive a BMW to DC
Sport some DKNY in LA

Gon' get away from the South
Get me some letters behind my name
Buy me some fortune
Earn my fame

Ain't gon' be nobody's maid.
Cuz my schooling made me smart
Got enough sense not to spend
time cleaning houses.

Got me some letters on the wall
though no letters to grandma.
No letters home, but she waits
for my return.

She knowd I would make it.
Made it cuz she didn't wait.
Made her money with lye soap
and rusty wash boards;
made my tuition in the kitchen.

Cast iron frying pans
cradle bacon grease.
Urine splattered toilet seats
saw her face everyday.
Jealous eyes prayed her hips
had not stained their sheets.

She… just a maid

Cuz she didn't wait to be a teacher
or knowledge seeker
She waits now though.
Can't close her eyes
'til she can see me.
See what she made.

At the Cross
for Carl

Middle seat on the alter be empty
be empty like my heart.

He gone
No good bye
No warning
He gone
Didn't wanna leave
Didn't have to leave

They sit and marvel.

They be like butchers to me-
carved up my soul

They be like thieves to me-
stole my delight

They be like Satan to me-
sought to devour me

They grin now.
They cheer now.
They leap now.

no kiss
no silver
no crown

But they
judged him
pierced him
crucified him

Can't go back
Can't look back
Can't reach back

Back is the cross.
Cross is his heart.
His heart is there.

But he gone.

Death

Ever seen death?
Looked at its wrath?
Smooth criminal takes forms
and steals like Jordan on the court.

Everything is fine when the culprit--
cancer
diabetes
AIDS--
creeps in uninvited and lifts
the soul from the body of our
mothers
fathers
sisters
brothers
lovers.

Or perhaps the crime is not premeditated-
a drunk driver
an unnamed bullet
or an unseasoned pilot may be the defendant.

Theft's effect is only understood by victims.

I remember my days as an observer
at the scene of the final viewing.
Lakes, valleys,
and rivers ran wild
on the faces of families.

All week long, folks had been over at the house,
bringing homemade German Chocolate cakes
and frying spicy Southern style chicken
for all the family who would be

in and out during that time.
And everyone seemed content
as they sipped on sweet iced tea
or ate plates and plates of cabbage
and potato salad that the lady
down the street had made.

News flash: "Death Stopped By"

The initial news headline prompts tears.
The days in between then and *that day*
are packed with so many pork chops,
"I'm sorrys",
and "I remember whens"
Weeping waits to arrive.

News flash: "The Funeral"
(weeping may begin)

Investigation complete
Report filed
Case closed
Free time to sit
Ponder the offense

That day has passed.
The food stops.
Company stays at home.

Alone…..
You hear the voice,
feel the touch of the hand
and see the body rocking in the chair.

Alpha and Omega.

Countdown

Big hand points to twelve.
Small hands points to seven.
It's time.

Two faint taps on the door,
followed by an sudden snatch
at my ankles with a recurrent
shout of "Wake up!"
It's just my alarm clock.

Through some miraculous perfection of routine,
I conduct a quick chemical experiment:
coalesce $H2O$ and soap.
I complete my fashion combo
and make it to my car in record time.

Five minutes later,
Beep beep at Joy's house.
Her fashion taste reflects on me:
Stone-washed Jordache jeans
A red and white turtle neck sweater
White Reebok tennis shoes with red shoe strings
Best friends do it better.

Cruise....
route one leads us to enjoy
chili dogs smothered in onions and coleslaw.
Cruise....
route two brings us to the traditional
homemade buttermilk biscuits filled
with country sausage patties.
Today- route one.

Our arrival is always surprisingly timely.

Walking down the halls,
we acknowledge the friendly remarks:
"Look at the Boppsie Twins"
"Y'all look like sisters."

First bell resonates and I am the first
to reserve a space in first period.
I arrive on time for reasons not
related to study:
I hide behind the biggest guy
in the class so that I can
consume my now cold hot dog.

Time ticks with pop quizzes
on *Wuthering Heights*
and lunch fights ensue
and couples break up
and friends make up
and the last bell sounds.

As head of the class,
we head out first.
First we visit the lockers
before we greet the visitors.
Although, Greg's no visitor to me cause
he stops by every day.
Greg departs after we share
a sensual sensation sparked by
the fusion of our lips.

Five o'clock comes and I punch the time clock.
I wonder, "Does Tom Smith realize
blue and yellow polyester is not the rave?"
Lincolns, Jacksons, and Washingtons
line the counter as I balance the register.
Hours pass without disturbance

when a customer returns to the store.
"Your cashier overcharged me!"

The clock shows eleven thirty and I'm done.
Though the hour is late, my arrival for home
is interrupted by a detour to Greg's house.
Tip tip
I catch a glimpse of Arsenio.
Stealing one hour, we explore
politics of the French
trends in lingerie
and the durability of a new mattresses.

At one a.m., I make my
way to my bed.
Thoughts of the next day
swirl my dome:
I can do second period's homework in first period-
third period's home work in…..
Sleep commences.

One hundred seventy five days later,
drops of "It's over!"
"We made it!"
and "What's next?"
find their way down our cheeks
drips from our chins
drizzles on our gowns.
It's the last dance.
Farewell to red ink filled exams
and long days of in-school suspension.

I grip my tassel,
envision the entire
and era in a matter of seconds.
My heart smiles.

Cuz We Country

Crickets talk about the
strong scent of honeysuckle.
Mosquitoes rob
the Red Cross blind.
Rattlesnakes shake tambourines to the tune
of "Jesus on the Main Line."

Hurricane rains bathe
stained pigs and rank horses.
Lightening bugs spotlight spider webs
putting on a spinning show.

Green lizards greet field mice
and see how they run.

Summertime is always
better in the country.

Fat back rests on pan fried
sweet onion cornbread.

Salmon croquettes snuggle close
beside the warmth of dirty rice.

Chitlins pass gas and scare the
liver pudding into a sac.

Homemade potato salads chills; no need
to sweat the technique.

Sweet potato pie and
Red Velvet cake dessert
the kitchen before sundown.

Deep fried mullets and spots drown
in Texas Pete.

Pickled pig's feet push pork rinds
out of their space in the cupboard.

Mealtime tastes better
in the country.

Warm castor oil
smoothes the cold away.

A raw onion on the feet
gives a fever the boot.
Brown paper bag in the roof
of the mouth shelters nose bleed.

Toothpaste protects skin
decay when chicken pox come
your way.

Clorox kills ring worms
and buries them in the ground..

Illness needs no physician
in the country.

How It Used to Be

When I'm away visiting grandparents,
they tell me how it used to be.
And although I wasn't around back then,
those things still seem important to me.

They tell me about the cotton fields,
picking as early as the break of day.
Their masters didn't care about backaches.
They weren't concerned in any way.

They tell me about shared bedrooms,
sometimes five to seven in a bed
If they were unhappy with that,
they could sleep outside instead.

They tell me about outdoor plumbing
and outhouses we now call commodes.
But that wasn't too far back
because even I have seen one of those.

They tell me about segregation,
bathrooms for Blacks and some for Whites.
We always got the run down ones
which didn't seem to be right.

They tell me about the movies.
Blacks had to sit upstairs.
The white people sat under us.
That too did not seem fair.

They tell me about pinto beans.
At times, that was all they had to eat.
But all the time they praised God
for they had a floor under their feet.

They tell me about the family car.
How crowded it used to be.
Everyone was on everyone else.
Phrases were heard like "Get off me!"

They tell me about the money
they had to spend on a summer's day.
Fifty cents isn't much to me,
but to them it went a long way.

They tell me about getting wood.
That's all they had to keep warm.
All had to help with this chore
in every way, shape, and form.

They tell me about the names
they were called over the years.
Words like "nigger" and "boy"
brought to their faces a myriad tears.

They tell me about some things
that I don't quite understand.
So I prayed to God for wisdom.
I told Him to take my hand.

When I'm away visiting grandparents,
they tell me how it used to be.
But that was then and this is now.
And a promising future awaits me.

Mother May I?

Wilted skin shelters the soul,
Blue veins branch out
from the root of her heart

She…
She, the "A" in the alphabet soup
that fed us knowledge of self

She, the concrete slab
that was our foundation

She…
Blue black
Sun kissed
Double-dipped chocolate
Texas tea tinged

She…
Like Cleopatra
Sheba
Nerfertiti

I knew her not though
and she fought so
I would not know
her journey of hot snow.

Ashes to ashes

"Mother, may I"
my thoughts cry
"May I
die?

Not Fair

When I was a young girl growing up
I remember thinking,
"I wish that I was white.
Then I would have long straight hair."
But my hair was nappy
and it just wasn't fair.

I also remember thinking,
"I wish I wasn't so dark.
Instead I wish my skin were lighter.
Then I could go to the beach
and lay out as if I didn't care."
But I couldn't and it wasn't fair.

Sometimes I used to think,
"I wish I were a lot thinner."
Instead my butt always stuck out.
I'd go shopping for cute little jeans
though most of them, I couldn't wear.
It was my big hips and it wasn't fair.

Then I got older and I remember thinking,
"I'm glad my hair is so thick.
I can braid it, curl it, dread it- whatever
I can make people stop and stare."
There's nothing special about a limp mane
and I guess that's just not fair.

When I look in the mirror
I think to myself
"I'm glad I don't have to get a tan.
The deep cocoa richness I was blessed with
Is a beauty that is uniquely rare."

Some people get cancer trying to look like me,
and I suppose that's not fair.

When I slip into some jeans
I think to myself, "Baby got back."
I never wonder if I'll be mistaken for a man.
To my curvaceous hips, a long back with a crack
cannot compare.
And who cares if it's not fair.

THE JUICE

My Country

My country is to me
sweet land of bigotry
I strongly detest.
Land where my fathers cried
ancestors, victims of genocide
from every countryside
Blacks remain oppressed.

My native country? Please…
land of the pure White free
thy name I loathe.
I loathe thy biased decrees
and every hypocrisy.
Will these injustices cease
or do we just hope?

A Dream I Had

Martin Luther King had a dream of harmony
and equality among all races.

The dream I had paints a future of peace and love
among people with Black faces.

The dream I had was a vision of the Black community
engaged in living together, free and full of love of our
flesh in all its natural hues.

This vision unveiled the shocking news story that Black
on Black love was at an all-time high, and overcrowding
in our places of worship had risen to record numbers.

Yes, I had a dream.

The dream I had unveiled the new cable station: BEN,
Black Edutainment Network. I saw people watching old episodes
of *The Cosby Show* and *Good Times,* embracing our diverse
heritage.

The dream I had showed Black-owned businesses
becoming victims of Benjamin bombardment
as we invested money in our own.

Black entertainers taking a cut in pay
to raise the standard of our images in the media.

Black voters electing to exercise their rights
and choosing a voice
that would speak the truth about what we need
what we want
and who we are.

I had a dream.

I saw a day when Black America disagreed
with the notion that we
must choose between Malcolm or Martin,
Booker T. or W.E.B.,
Jackson or Sharpton.
Instead, we supported all of these leaders,
taking from each one a truth check and depositing that check
in our homes, hearts, and community until enough interest
had grown to reinvest.

Yes, that was the dream I had. Then I woke up to the nightmare
that is reality
which reveals us wasting Franklins on Tommy
cause Shae Shae and Little Man sportin Calvin Klein
and we can't let them out do us.

I woke up to the tragedy of Black folk
putting each other down.
Instead of pulling one another up by the boot straps,
we are stepping on each other with our boots,
brothers giving our children the boot
and sisters giving up the booty to every Tom,
Dick, and Malik.

I woke up to the fallacy that a white woman
on a Black man's arm is worth more
than a Black woman who has his back.
The mentality that too many Black women
believe the way to their heart
should be through a Black man's wallet.

This nightmare revealed the heart wrenching agony
that there are more Black men in jail
than Black men in homes with their children.

I saw the scary scene of Black kids reciting songs
from Jay Z and Nelly,
but they were forgetting the words
to The Lord's Prayer.

Today, there is a nightmare on our street,
and it's not Freddy with the knife.
We are killing ourselves.

We inject into our veins music
which suggests our self image is shaped
by women, cars, and ice.

We allow cancerous tumors of hate
between light skin sisters and
dark skin sisters to grow in our bodies.

We die of heart failure because we're not allowing
enough love to grow within ourselves to speak
to one another and greet one another. And not knowing
how to function without love, our hearts just stop.

Dead End on a One Way Street

Caramel coated eyes locked on me,
secure like dentures bonded on pink gums
in Big Mama's mouth.

Honey brown glow radiated from his face.
Quicksand thick lips had me stuck in thoughts
of "Who he be?"

Me,
Flo Jo quick to grab the
baton and relay my thoughts
to his heart.

Common interests in law
made the case to exchange digits:
Cell
Fax
Home
Pager
Work

Strong man I saw
Boy child he was
Sweet too
Not sweet like thoughtful deeds of rose petals
placed on pillows and sheets...

He was sweet like Little Richard
trapped in an Invisible life.

My gaydar picked up faint signals that
stopped me at a long red light.
Stuck in traffic
trapped by compassion,

tricked by deception
No need to get
burnt on a stove to know it's hot.

Wanting to make sure it
was heat I felt and not
my own insecurities burning within
I thought I would keep it friendly.

The weak signal still remained.

Can't go on
Can't go back
So I sit here.

Colors

I like colors.

Colors like the majestic reverence in red and white.
Colors that glow in the thick of night.

I like colors.

Colors that rap the round fullness of my natural lips.
Colors that embrace the eclipse of my moon-dipped hips.

I like colors.

Colors like soft brown walnut
and gentle silk buttercup.

Colors that blind the bright pearl and molars and cuspids that bite.

Colors new and true
encompassing and encircling

Colors
Colors
Like my people

Like the cream-filled chocolate children on the block
and cinnamon hard bodes like my man, The Rock.

I like colors.

Colors of Harriet and Martin
Malcolm and those forgotten.

Colors that dripped with the sweat of Denmark Vessey.
Colors that haunted Ferguson vs. Plessy.

Colors
I like colors.
Colors of the rainbow
Colors of my people
The colors of the rainbow comprise the colors of my people.

Every color in the rainbow is found in the colors of my people
The colors of the rainbow
The colors of my people

Colors
I like colors
The colors are my people.

Little Black Girl

There once was a little Black girl,
whose dreams were high as the sky.
She had many goals she wanted to achieve
and she planned to give each a try.

As a child, she had a lot of interests.
She wanted to be in everything.
Once she auditioned to play Patti LaBelle
and she knew she couldn't sing.

As she grew older, her interests blossomed.
Suddenly she noticed a big change.
In school, she and her white classmates
were not always treated the same.

Junior high came and she was growing up.
Her knowledge of life was growing too.
She continued to be faced with racism
no matter what she tried to do.

She began to recall the many struggles
her people had fought over the years.
She knew they had given their lives
for they had conquered so many fears.

With that in mind, she set a new goal
cause she knew God was on her side.
She marched with her head held high
and soon discovered Black Pride.

With Black Pride, she soared forward.
Little Black girl was ready for the test.
She knew no matter the obstacles,
she was destined to be a success.

This little Black girl became a woman
with the motto, "Be all you can be."
I know she's living up to it too
because she lives inside of me.

Today as a woman, I am blessed.
I have the chances others were denied.
I owe it to those who paved the way
to reverence the front seat ride.

Sticks and Stones

What can I say to heal the hurt?
help clean the dirt
thrown on your face
by those considered your friends

What can I do to erase the memory?
that night of flying sticks and debris,
the soulful snippets of self shame
when tattletales smeared your name.

Memories make it hard to forget
and even harder to forgive.
Yet we continue to relive
and we keep looking back
reminiscing on every attack,
recalling our mistakes,
remembering the problems we make.

All have come short.
Still, all need support.
Everyone falls victim to stones
and every one needs time to atone.

What do you need to hear?
to realize assistance is near,
to know that love surrounds you,
that it's time to begin anew

I have lain in the bed you've made.
I almost drowned in the waters you wade.
I know the taste of broken trust.
I know the smell of self disgust.

Sticks and stones do break bones
but words can break the heart.

So use the words to help you heal.
Employ those words to change how you feel.
Take those sticks as a staff for support.
Use the stones to build your own fort.
Stick to the vision placed in your soul.
Stone the hurt within and make your heart whole.

Broken bones heal themselves in time.
To heal the heart, you must restore the mind.

Waiting to Excel

No money right now
Can't go back to school
'Sides Lil Mama needs new clothes

Start my new business next year
Boss wants me on a special project
No time to research my market plans

Need to get organized with my papers
'Fore I send you a proposal
When I move next year, I'll set up the office

Gotta buy my own computer
to format and revise my book
The library too far to drive to every day

Wait until the children are grown
Then I can invest in a new sound system
Mixing records in their old bedrooms

No time for cheerleading this year
Need to go home to clean the house
I should loose weight anyway

I won't go the movie audition
Old headshots don't look like me
Plus, the studio is a long drive from home

I'll try out for football next year
after I work out over the summer.
Then I know I'll make the team.

Why wait?
Tomorrow will bring with her new stuff:

More bills
Different problems
Jealous friends
Demanding bosses
Broken relationships
Chronic illnesses
Emergency phone calls

Fear tells us that we should wait
But fear never won a game
He hasn't started a business
And fear knows no success

Closed doors are made to be knocked down
Opportunity sometimes resembles defeat
Winners don't loose the lesson
You can't rise if you're still in your seat
You can't rise if you're not on your feet
You can't run if you're not in the game
You can't win if you're not in the game
You can't win if you're afraid to lose
You can't win if you never choose

Why wait for chance when you can work for choice?
Visualize the prize. Actualize with your voice.

A New Declaration

When in the course of inhumane events
it becomes crucial that the oppressed,
break the umbilical cord
connecting them with those in power,
and assume a new status of empowerment
and affluence which is entitled
by virtue of their citizenship,
acknowledgment of the backlash
from the Majority necessitates
that they should proclaim
their reasons for severance.
Jefferson himself declared that
"all men are created equal
with certain unalienable rights-
Life, Liberty, and the Pursuit of Happiness."
But these rights have dangled on a string
in the faces of blue collar workers,
people of color, and the poor communities
caught up in the struggle.

Unemployment is currently on the rise,
while poor families face a needless demise.
Corporate bailouts are served from Bush's menu,
as cuts in social programs continue.
We the *people* of the United States,
declared war on the evil leaders of terrorism.
While at home, tax breaks and miscounted votes
enforce our country's institutionalized racism.
This new war has made daily living tougher
and the poor and working class continue to suffer.
This axis of evil extends beyond the Middle East
for evil has become our country's centerpiece.
Money is the focus of this current upheaval.
And the love of money is the root of all evil.

America, the beautiful? Oh, I think not.
Slavery, lynchings, you thought we forgot?
O wicked men who dehumanized
for growth on their terrain,
and sheets that covered deceitful eyes,
helped keep their stolen rein.
America, America, God shed disgrace on thee
And frowns upon what you have done,
to the slaves who worked for free.
We must separate ourselves before the boomerang returns.
Everyone reaps what he sows,
but America still hasn't learned.
We must declare our independence from the Divided States.
And claim our freedom to control our fate.
We shall overcome, not someday, but now.
They can only do what we passively allow.
It's time for a revolution and not one of war:
a revolution in our spirit, where we say, "No more!"
No more cuts in education or rising costs in health care.
No more ostracizing our brothers and sisters on welfare.
No more miscounted votes when we exercise our rights.
No more jail time for Blacks with mere probation for Whites.
War is the tool of the enemy. Faith is our steadfast friend.
United we make a difference.
Divided we continue the trend.
No justice. No peace. But in justice, there's peace.
Just for us, pieces of anticipation
for our own emancipation proclamation.
Thus, we demand our freedom in the midst of war.
We sing our victory song to the One we adore.
Free at last, to work and be treated fair.
Free at last, to claim our rightful share.
Thank God Almighty is the song to be sung.
For we recognize that power lies in the tongue.
So we stand united in this freedom affirmation.
Giving notice to all of this the new declaration.

MELLOW MURMURS

Mirror Mirror

He be like Now & Laters
and mayonnaise sandwiches
Monday after school;
recollections of lemons
swimming in red Kool-aid
in a Mt. Olive Pickle jar.

He, like crimson silk sheets laced in
baby powder
with the woo woo woo of Osborne's
tenor dancing in my ear.
Salt water waves
tickling the arch of my back,
saturating my inner thigh,
and nestling beside my pinky toe.

He be like playing double dutch
jump rope
before Ms. Mary Mack
and Ms. Lucy's steamboat
sailing by Hopscotch
boxes and Mother May I lines.

He be like…..
me.

Me.
I am to him like collard greens and
crackling bread with sweet potato pie
sitting on a plate waiting to be
joined by hoop cheese baked with
macaroni and canned milk.

Me, the fragrant aroma of

Chanel No. 5 coalesced by the
natural chemistry of my
36-24-39,
and caressed by
licorice thongs
a lace brassiere
and a jet black garter.

Me, the baby doll head
propelled by his bat
sending him to second base.
Scratched up metal wheels
on black pleather skates,
the .38 Special grasped by
his G.I. Joe right before battle
as he makes a mad dash
for his Incredible Hulk Big Wheel.

We indeed connect four.

For better
For worse
For richer
For poorer

Me and he,
reflections of reciprocal
emulations, more than
an imitation of life, though
less than perfect.

Red Light Special

The soothing sound of Luther Vandross seeps seduction
in the room as the adrenaline teems to titillation
and reaches a peak.
The temples heat as the ticking increases to full bloom,
and the playful petals of perspiration roll down
during the first shriek.
The satin sheets slyly show the silky ever-changing shapes,
as the springs of the Sealy Posturepedic begin to squeak.
The running rivers of passion rivet through the trembling gate
while the continuous undulation of the cork appears not to cease.
The obtrusive outburst of painful pleasure is impossible to ignore.
As the melodious moans commence to decrease,
the sound of Luther's soulful and sensual selection is heard once more.

Ghost
for Randy

Casper disappears then reappears.
Who you gonna call?

Who can I call to get you back?

No *69 or call forwarding to connect us
I reach out and touch. You gone.

Cell phone still stores all seven digits.
Email files messages of "What's up. Let's talk soon."

My heart still stores your voice.

Some glad morning, we all vanish.
Your morning was yesterday,
and today I hurt because every tomorrow
will be without you.

I blink.

Third eye films produce clairvoyant movie
starring you as yourself.

Your salt and pepper crown
creates a seasoned halo.

Benjamins become Lincolns
Notes stamped past due prompt paper ads:
SBM seeks boarder.
Boarder brings bad babes who
burns bed

The face off brews battles

Blood clot block speech
Robbed heart beat stopped.

I blink.

The last role for you.

No more Meisner
I audition
No more classes
I project
No more….

An Intimate Disclosure Session
for Poopy

As I sat on the couch, which was my usual ritual
in the afternoon, my mind was quickly consumed
as my remote control
became the vehicle I used to roll
between Oprah Boulevard,
Springer Drive, and Rickie Road. But this day,
I decided to take a detour from the
usual route and headed off in pursuit of Maury's Street
and parked there while I kept my seat.

There was a man I saw who was just like me.
Billy was his name and
Russian Roulette was his game.
He lost just as I had and he was left
feeling alone and sad.
I sat listening to him explain how
it all began for him, while my mind
went back to the night I met Jim.

Jim was tall with a smile that could
blind Stevie Wonder. The depth of his
voice filled oceans of desire within me
and made me realize that image was nothing
and thirst was everything. Or, so I thought.

Days became weeks and I no
longer had the strength to deny
my pearl its pleasure principle.
We shared an intimate disclosure
session so close that there was no
need for our *Lifestyle* to get in the way.
(I still regret that day.)

Jim and I had no formal agreement,
no contracts, or stipulations binding
us to one another. We were free
agents and he chose to play the game
whenever he had a chance to get
up to bat. I have no idea how many times he
scored, but the scars from all those
homeruns found their way into my home
and I can no longer run away from their mark.

Fast forward to the present and I
listened to Billy admit that his intimate disclosure
session did not happen through intercourse but through
an interchange of highs. Tears ran down his face
and I realized I had to leave Maury's place
because the pain of my scars began to
rear their ugly face.
I scrolled along to Oprah Boulevard
as Dr. Phil revealed the skills
needed to maintain a healthy
relationship with your significant other
and I thought, "Not another sappy love story."

So I got on the road again, but
everywhere I saw the lesson I had learned,
(too late) and I thought of my fate,
as I knew my time to expire
did not even comprise an entire
year. Still, I did not fear,
for I knew within my heart,
my life was only the start,
and someday soon, a loosing
game of Russian Roulette would
not cast a cloud of doom, but simply
convey an important lesson of using wisdom
in an intimate disclosure session.

Heavy Heart
for Brown Sugar

My heart is heavy tonight.

My heart is heavy tonight
because I'm holding a love that I can't let go,
that I can't let show
that he can never know.

My heart is heavy tonight.

What I see in this man
is nothing and everything at the
same time.

He's a maple syrup dipped morsel
of caramel and milk chocolate sundae.

We hooked up on a business project.
No desire to blend business with pleasure or
have him measure my mind by my behind.
The choice to remain voiceless was made.

Besides, pride and fear blocked arteries
won't let blood flow to my heart.
Won't let this love get its start.

So, I hold it all in
hoping the passion will end.

But destiny knows no U-turn.

I see my soul in his smile,
and daydream in Surround Sound on 20 by 40 feet screens
in movie theaters.

He is my leading man. I am his leading lady.
He's more than a *best man*.
Sweeter than *brown sugar*. Sanaa Lathan and Taye Diggs can't match us together.
We make *the best brown sugar in the wood*.
I mean, I wish we could.

But I can't.
And my heart is heavy tonight.

I feel his presence in my breath.

Spending time with him lets me know
it's not about finding the right person
but being the right person.
And I want to be the right to his left,
the up to his down,
the smile for his frown.
I want to be the light in his soul.
I want to give light 'til he glows.

I'm bent over with this weight
that's breaking my back
that's bending my spine.
It's invading my mind.

Cause my heart is heavy tonight.

I'm carrying this love that I can't let go
that I can't show
that he can never know.

And destiny knows no U-Turn.

I hear his voice in my heartbeat and see my potential in his weakness.

He's not a perfect man. But he practices what he preaches.
Practice makes perfect and perfect practice makes perfection.
So together we can perfect the practice of perfection.

When I run my finger under my nose, I'm reminded of cinnamon
sticks, gingerbread houses, and lilac and lavender mists. And
that's from the handshake he gave me two weeks ago. His scent
lingers on me like garlic on the breath of the nail shop lady.

I see our wedding in my fantasies
and our children in my dreams.
I taste his salt in my tears.
I feel my strength in his fears.

I see Jesus in him.
I feel Jesus in me and since Jesus is love,
what stronger love could there be?
I know it was meant to be. He was God sent to me.
I want to think that it could be.

But he'll never know cause I can't let it show.

And my heart is heavy tonight.

He inspires me to be my best self;
not pretend to be
or dress up to be
but be the best I can be.
He inspires me to be all
that I can be and I want to be an Army
of one with him, fighting enemy
fire with the fullness of our faith.

But I can't let this go.
I can't let this show.

He can never know.

So my heart is heavy tonight.
Cause destiny knows no U-turn.

Poetry

Paper as a safe ocean
dry ink spots thirst for a well
of warm moisture to douse the spark.

Words as rivers, wide and welling in the sun
strides of setting moons and rising comets.

Sonnets and limericks as kindred foes
dancing on rhymes and forms of meter
burning embers of coals in backyard
grills on June nineteenth

Poetry to me-paper and ink
consummating a sacred relationship
old in spirit
fresh by design.

Sunset
Chincoteague Island, VA

Hair gently swaying from the force of
nature off the waters

The sky's reflection mirrored upward to
the heavens, forming a Siamese junction on
the shore.
It captivates
It calms.
Bellows from geese mellowed
by the distant beams crawling across the bridge
falling in and out of view behind the fence.

The high and low speeds blink
a 70's disco beat.
The horizon reveals the yellow daughters
of the dust,
the red man native to the land,
the orange fire that blazes between
white ice and black coal.
the purple people whose colors
so deep it drowns those who attempt to steal its glow.

The blue days ahead for the children
whose emergency call for help
was disconnected by 911.

The low clouds creep by
on their way to the east.

The sunset.

Beauty only wishes she
had half of your presence.

Beating the Blues
for Y

My daddy taught me about the blues.
Not the blues of Miles and his horn
engaged in a hot and heated lip lock
producing melodic climaxes.

My daddy taught me about the blues of the Mississippi River,
its waters waging war with the bodies of Black leaders and
teachers.

My daddy taught me about the blues of watching his daddy
being stripped of his manhood
as he closed his mouth and stood.
For nothing could be said when daddy's mama
wept and bled from a white man's genital intrusion.

My daddy taught me about the blues: the Black man's blues.

Sometimes at night, my brother and I woke up to the sight
of my Mama's face, black and blue from the blows that he threw.
How could he beat my mother when she was his lover?

I would cry when I saw how badly she was bruised.
Mama never worried. She said he was just beating the blues.

I saw the skin that was torn from the wounds
that were worn on her face, and I thought it was a disgrace.
But one day my mama told us the Bible says,
"Wives submit yourselves to your own husband."

That's why she never raised a hand
each night when the beating began.

I couldn't understand how my daddy

could kiss the bruises he created;
rub the back that he mutilated;
enter the womb that he brutally attacked;
caress the ribs that his feet had cracked.

My mama died very young; people weren't shocked at the news.
It wasn't diabetes or cancer; she died from a Black man's blues.

I thought back to my daddy as I laid in a hospital brace.
I'm married now and I understand a woman's place.

My husband, Mike, knows about daddy's blues.

Mike taught me about the blues
of lights that blind and shine in rearview mirrors
and sirens that ring out in the middle of the night,
charging him once again with DWB,
and it's sad to me, but that's his reality.

Mike didn't mean to hurt me when kicked me with his shoes.
I realize he's just a Black man, beating the blues.

There are days when I want to stand up like Little Boy Blue
and blow my horn on the thorn that is in my side.
Cause I don't know how long I can hide the black and blue scars
that pad my face and the rips that line the lips of my holy space.
That's how I got pregnant in the first place.

My baby was the one thing I didn't want to lose.
I know it was an accident, cause he was just beating the blues.

Yes, I get tired of cuts and the agony of neglect.
I've heard the whisk of his belt as it lashes my neck.
I've felt the pain of the swollen joints that support my spine.
I've seen the open sores along my waist line.
I've smelled the pus that oozes from my open wounds.

I've tasted the blood from a fetus that arrived far too soon.
Though when given an option, Mike is what I would always choose.
For better or for worse, I know in my heart he's just beating the blues.

Dark Star

Well-dressed sentences like
a fresh flounder at a fish fry
formed from his lips.

They danced in ripples of pulsating
vibrations penetrating her inner ear
to the melody of *do re mi.*

Soft scents of cologne fondled
the hairs in her nostrils
and stroked the spine of her back

And when he was not there, she could
smell his presence in her breath.

They kissed.

She saw stars.

She saw stars.

She saw stars that formed a constellation shaped like a heart
with the continent of Africa at its center.
His words were an extension of her thoughts.

Chocolate-coated lips making her ask herself,
"What would I do for a Klondike bar?"

His hands held her heart.
The brotha was her feng shui.

Baby love was her cozy cup of coffee in the morning.
He was good to the last drop and the best part
of waking up was a little dash of him in her cup.

His shine would blind but his dark would mark
days of solitude
nights of thunderstorms.
The sky cries
and drips tears
on the forest floor of her heart.

His dark side was down though
made her frown so

Down like Mary J after KC
down like four flat tires on a low rider
down like the Blues of B.B. and Lucille when
the thrill is no longer real.

No sound in his voice
no shine in his smile
no glow from his soul
His light fades....

Forbidden Fruit

When I look into your eyes,
I see my soul.

We are indeed one:

one mind,
one body
one spirit,
one love

My thoughts are filled with thoughts
of you and you fill me
completely
effortlessly.

When we talk, my mind leaves my body,
joining your mind in the blue seas of South Beach,
where together they merge and create
magical metaphors, astonishing assonance
lively alliteration, among other things.

And yet, you are off limits.
In the here and now
there is no place for you in my life.

But my eyes can see the man who lives
just below the surface of the rough neck
punk you so proudly project.

Strawberries,
kiwis,
and mangos
are thought to be fruits of passion.

But it is you, my forbidden fruit,
for which my mouth waters,
my stomach craves,
my heart desires,
and my spirit yearns.

Black History

Bestowing
Legacies
And
Chronicles
Kept
Hidden
In
Statements
That
One-sidedly
Recorded
Yesterday

The Black Family Prevails

Though bought, stolen and sold,
Tortured in ways to horrid to detail,
Though separated from mother and father,
The Black Family still prevails.

They may have robbed us of our language,
Falsely imprisoned our men in jail,
They labeled our children as slow.
Yet, the Black Family fruitfully prevails.

They have cheated us of our wages;
Raped us, with no one else to tell.
They took credit for our inventions.
But the Black Family undoubtedly prevails.

They dragged our brothers to their deaths;
Leaving innocent blood as their trail.
They gave us drugs to kill our own.
By God's grace, the Black Family prevails.

We have turned brother against brother.
Daughters rising against their mothers,
Friends fighting other friends,
Relatives at war with their kin.

In spite of our self inflicted pain,
When our foundation seems so frail,
We find strength deep within our roots
And the Black Family continues to prevail.

We may get drunk and fight.
And feud all hours of the night.
Amazingly, comes the peace of a dove.
The Black Family is unconditional love.

We never received our forty acres.
Sometimes, we're left waiting to exhale.
And even without our reparations,
The Black Family somehow prevails.

Across the morbid middle passages,
Through hundreds of years of slavery,
Surviving the Black Codes and segregation,
The Black Family equates bravery.

We stay together because we pray together.
So, when all of man's solutions fail.
Many will be lost to revolting tribulation.
But the Black Family will always prevail.

LIGHT VIBES AND SPOKEN WORD

Prelude to a Kiss

For weeks we had several intimate conversations.
We talked about many different situations.
And as the day drew near of "the occasion,"
I soon started to sense a sensual sensation.

We were business associates.
Friendly business associates
More like friends
More than friends

A love of the arts enticed us
as we debated Spike, John,
and Oprah too.
Never once did we stop to notice the incredible
magnetism that was connecting
our minds
our hearts
and our souls.

Perhaps I did notice the subtle allusions
as you often suggested
behind the guise of business,
that you and me
should become we.

Perhaps I recognized the sly indications
as you mentioned one day out of the blue
"I can't talk to her the way I talk to you."

Maybe I perceived the skillful hints you made
and wondered exactly how it could be,
as you used my friend to spend time talking to me.

Maybe I sensed your crafty style
as you casually made me aware,
that when you saw my sexy legs they
stimulated your entrancing stare.

Maybe I suspected your unconcealed affection
as you took my hand in the club and massaged your face,
and sat there for a few seconds
clinched in a gentle embrace.

Perhaps I discerned your fading mask
as you helplessly gazed into my eyes,
making one of those distinct passes
while I sat there wearing your glasses.

Perhaps I knew it was inevitable
as you locked me in your car,
prolonging the date
prolonging the wait.

And then it happened.
Our lips finally touched.

At first I backed away,
but realized I wanted to stay
stay there in that moment
stay there with you.

When our lips touched again,
something magical, magnetic, and momentous occurred.
I felt you, not just on my lips.
but I **FELT** you.

As your tongue gently glided with mine,
I felt you touching me, unclothing me,
revealing a desire that had been hiding within me.

As you passionately bit my lip,
I felt you touching me, taking Cupid's scalpel
cutting deep into my skin
revealing my heart,
revealing my soul.

And as I erotically kissed you back,
I once again felt you touching me.
I felt you exposing me.
I felt you touch my spirit.

It was a simple pair of glasses that allowed us to see
the volatile chemical experiment that we had become.

But things are quite complicated
although your heart is not truly dedicated.

Maybe I'm just a number on your list,
for Judas betrayed Jesus with a kiss.
So there is no way I can dismiss
that a hidden agenda does not exist.

Or maybe you too sit and reminisce
about the night of our first kiss.
Perhaps your eyes fill with mist
as you ponder our metamorphosis.

Maybe it was just a kiss.
Maybe it was more.
God only knows
what our future has in store.

Only time will tell if the intimate moment we shared
has planted the seeds that through

time, care and growth
will bloom into the perfected petals of love.

A Fallen Hero

How could it be?
You and she,
becoming we
abandoning family
so selfishly.

Had you fantasized
about her thighs
and the surprise
her love would comprise?

What were you thinking
when you kissed her breast
and her body you caressed,
when her lips touched your chest?
Could you not withstand the test?

Was it a mistake?
Or an act of fate?

Happenstance
or
Circumstance

Was it really a must
to concede to your lust
and break your wife's trust?

A mistake, you say,
but it's an affair I see
when you and she
became we.

And all the while,
you continued to smile
and walked the last mile
and endured your trials
in the midst of your beguile.

For you, I had respect,
and I felt you would protect.
Now, in retrospect,
I wholeheartedly reject
your ploy to misdirect.

For you, I had the love
that heaven sent from above.
You decided to shove
that love away, just because.

You were once my hero.
That you should know.
Now it seems as though
I can no longer bestow
that title to you.

"How could you do it?" you ask.
I also find it hard to believe
that you and she
became we.

Am I truly able to forgive?
Or will I continue to relive
the act that was so deliberate
so derogative
so massive
just so....

One day I'll look into your eyes
and not have to visualize
your hands crawling up her thighs
as you heatedly begin to rise
and fertilize
the seed that stunted your growth.

Although evil was her motive,
I can't put the blame on her alone.
For she was not on her own
when you and she
became we.

My heart is saddened and I agonize
as you continue to apologize
about your affair in disguise.
And it is here that I should advise
that you have forfeited the prize,
for you are no longer my hero.

You were once my hero.
Now you're just a zero
all because you and she
became we.

I know one day I'll forgive
and that moment, I'll no longer relive.

For now I must
rebuild
repair
and restore.
After every storm, there is a rainbow.
Until then, I'll have one less hero.

Playing Your Fool

I just don't understand.
You weren't a real man.
You never held my hand.
But I was your biggest fan.
And I gave my love to you.

I gave the relationship many tries,
only to be bombarded with your lies.
And it's funny how time flies
when you think someone loves you.

You subjected me to so much ridicule.
And there I was, playing your fool.

Every night on my knees, I prayed.
And even though I was dismayed
in the relationship I stayed
thinking one day, children we would raise
constantly supporting you with praise.

I shared moments with you,
that I had never shared before.

And when I looked in your eyes,
I could sometimes visualize
the life we would one day share.

Monogamy? To you that wasn't "cool."
But I stayed there, playing your fool.

If I had a dollar for every
phone number,
rubber,
unexplained gift,

cancelled date,
late night page,
lie, and let's not forget
the endless number of females.

If I had a dollar for every one of
your indiscretions....
I'd be chilling with Trump or Gates by now.
Swimming pools. Movie Stars.

Why did I stay?
Why couldn't I walk away?

Our time was filled with strife.
But I wanted you in my life,
even thought I'd be your wife,
but that couldn't be.
That shouldn't be.
It won't be.

How could all the candlelight dinners,
showers together,
weekend vacations,
breakfasts in bed,
skipped work days,
thoughtful gifts,
nights of love making,
spring picnics,
and evening backrubs
not keep us together?

I loved you.
There's no other way to say it.
I loved you.

I loved you completely,
freely,
honestly,
wholeheartedly,

Yet you walked over me like I was a footstool.
And with you I stayed, playing your fool.

Everyone plays the fool, that's what I hear.
Still that doesn't bring back the years
nor does it calm my fears

You destroyed my self-pride
and my face I attempted to hide,
while going along for the ride.
Yet now my eyes are open wide.
For God is still on my side.
He's always been my guide.
I just forgot to look to Him.
I forgot to let Him.
I forgot Him.

All the time I ran after you
thinking I knew what to do,
when actually I didn't have a clue.
For it was God I needed to pursue.
From His presence, I withdrew.
My walk with Him, I needed to renew.
A date with Him was overdue.

See, I had confused sin for affection,
thinking sex was the right selection,
forgetting God's plan for that connection–
the worship of oneness and perfection.
And fearing your harsh rejection
I posed no objection.

My temple, I did disregard.
And though I had a broken heart,
a new walk I will start.
So before I completely depart
I have some words I must impart.

I was a fool for you long ago.
Still, I think that you should know
you will reap what you sow.
But your soul, you shouldn't forgo.
Forgiveness God will still bestow.

Confession by mouth is His only rule.
So quit the stupid game of playing Satan's fool.

Chestnut Brown

I remember one morning watching the summer sunrise
in your eyes and the beauty they revealed was mesmerizing,
hypnotizing, and paralyzing as I found myself slowly drowning
in a hallucination of quicksand.

Unable to breathe with a love song caught in my throat,
I started to choke from the swelling that was dwelling within,
and then I realized without a doubt,
that love song had to come out.

Umm Umm Umm... I saw circles of starlight gates
leading the path along the underground railroad
to the essence of your soul. Your chestnut brown eyes
gently caressed the nape of my neck, sending a surge of static
down my spine, so electrifying that it's terrifying to know that this
stimulating romance began with just a glance.

Sometimes in the crescent moonlight, I see a sensual sparkle
in your eyes that chills my skin like a winter wind, but then
warms my presence like the moisture from a Mississippi well.

Your chestnut brown eyes round the curves of my flesh
and flicker like a flame recreating a volcanic eruption
in a Philippine forest.

You see, what you ignite in me is more powerful than a bolt
of lightning in a Carolina thunderstorm,
and yet and still, at will,
you can look at me again and then
cool my fire like the snow atop a peak at Grandfather Mountain.

I get intoxicated just from your glare, knowing
that if I stare too long, I will be well
over the legal limit of passion. But that's okay,

because a day or two behind bars could never
remove the stars in my eyes and my mind that were
formed while I was under the influence of chestnut brown.

There isn't a stream, river, lake, or ocean that could quench
the thirst I have for your eyes. Even when days have gone by
without seeing you, I stop, rewind, and playback in my mind
snippets of those precious pearls with dark pupils as they peered
at me. And immediately my thirst is extinguished.

As I reminisce on the tender night we shared a midnight walk
along the warm and wet waters of Wrightsville Beach,
with my third eye, I can still see
the way those chestnut browns looked at me.
My heart started beating to the rhythm of an African drum,
melodies of love ballads, freedom tunes, and Negro spirituals
all woven together in a song cycle that repeated itself
until I was completely seduced. With the blink of your eye,
I had fallen under the command of the man who is the HNIC-
"Head Nubian in Chestnut."

As I gaze in your eyes, I see my soul, my spirit filling
each part of you from the arch in your feet to the sweet
thrust of your manhood, feeling so good, and rounding
to the crown of your head, so it could no longer be said that you
and I are two, but instead one. For what had begun
as a summer fling has emerged into the real thing.
Just like the roundness of your eyes, having no beginning
or ending, so it is with me and you and me and you
and me and you....
or is it you and me?
I think you too can see that L word weaving us together
in an orbit with no origin or conclusion so that at the center of our
souls is a radiance that glows,
like your chestnut brown eyes.

An Independent Black Woman's Rebuttal

You say,

The Independent Black Woman
sifts the breath from your lips,
on your wallet, she tightly grips,
while you drown amidst her hips.

I say,
You have only experienced
hos and skeezas,
pocket squeezas.

You say,
The Independent Black Woman
has leaned on you,
schemed on you,
dumped dreams on you.

I say,
You have only crossed paths
with the ghetto girls
draped in diamonds and pearls
with thoughts of a material world.

You have only known perpetrators:
those who try to imitate
but fail to duplicate
the unique ambiance and royalty
that is the very essence of an
Independent Black Woman.

Just because she wore the suit
had the degree
talked the talk

drove the G.T.
and walked the walk
your eyes could only see the mask.
Your fragile ego was completely
destroyed because you could not
comprehend the fact that you had been...
PLAYED!!

You have never known an
Independent Black woman.

But because I like you,
I will take a moment to relate
and re-educate.
So don't make the mistake
of missing the point I make.

An Independent Black Woman is one
who loves herself
because she is herself
knows herself
respects herself
protects herself

There is no co-dependent necessity
to be with you or any other for
through her reciprocity
she is your equal.

She knows what she will accept
rejects that which disrespects
constantly nurtures her intellect
while her steps, the Lord directs.

She is one who can stand on her own
knowing she is never alone.

But she can lean on your love
while remaining strong enough
to be weak when she needs to be.

An Independent Black Woman
knows that giving love does
not involve sex,
and knows that making love
doesn't either.

She is the mahogany diva
whose head is never bowed
for her steps flow with a queenly stride,
a consequence of her African pride.

Her smile gleams with the self-assurance
that generations of women have instilled in her.

Her eyes sparkle with the love
that has grown from the seeds planted at her conception.

An Independent Black Woman knows
that she can be wrong, even
when she's right.

Her long legs are symbolic of the paths,
hills, and valleys that she has traveled
to arrive at the destination
at which God has blessed her to be.

Her spirit is undeniable as God's
presence shines through her very being;
for she knows she is independent
because she is dependent on Him.

You see,
you have never known An Independent Black Woman.

For if you had,
you would have taken the time to
know her
love her
embrace her.

Her very nature silently demands a
magnetism so powerful
so beautiful
so spiritual
that when you have tasted the chocolate
that envelops her, you will know
why blackberry juice is sweetest,
and your thirst for any other
simply won't exist.

butter beans
selling frozen cups
and lemonade
or helping with the chicken plates your aunt made.

Remember summer afternoons,
eating Sugar Babies
priming pumps to get a drink of water
picking plums and blackberries
eating sour weeds
and finding honeysuckles.

Take me back to the days of granddaddy
killing the hog on Friday,
so we could have bacon on Sunday,
while grandma wrung the neck on the chicken
and Aunt Lula Belle shelled peas
and Uncle Ray Ray was finishing
the moonshine that all the men
would drink that night.

Think about the days
of community closeness
quality family time
Cadillac's
side burns
Shaft
and Michael Jackson,
(when he had his real nose
his real chin
and he was still Black.)

Take me back to the days
of Hide and Go Get It
knowing who would get it
cause you hid where he got it the last time.

Take Me Back

Take me back to the days of Friday fish fries,
Saturday afternoons getting your hair straightened for church,
and partying Sunday night in the club owned by your uncle,
grubbing on oxtails and pig feet....
until granddaddy gets drunk and starts shooting
and runs everyone away.

Or Mr. Henry stopping by to get that
fifty-cent shot of liquor,
after school sitting around watching and experiencing
"Good Times"
"Different Stokes"
and "The Facts of Life"

Take me back to the summertime
playing with your cousins:
Mother May I,
Hopscotch,
Color Color Out,
1, 2, 3 Red Light,
Simon Says,
Jack Rocks,
or when daddy got paid
it was the Lemon Twist you played.

Or how about Grandma's homemade biscuits
with those sweet thick molasses,
real grits cooked in a pot,
with that air-dried sausage,
and fried green tomatoes.

Take me back to the days of making
money before your were old enough to work:
picking peas

Take me back. Take me back
before thugs were worshipped as the "Macs."
Today we pay our money at the rap shows
as the artist calls women, "freaks and hos."
We trade in food stamps for a new outfit
while our children are hungry and sick.
Making money by performing blows,
equating love with a bloody nose.
Going to the doctor to suck out that life
so we can still party every Saturday night
Giving of our spirit before commitment
carrying a sign that reads "Booty for rent."

We need to go back.

Take me back.
I want to go back.
We need to go back.
We should go back.
We must go back.
We have to go back.

To move forward
Move forward
We have to back
To move forward.

Reminisce on the days
of sacred living rooms,
where plastic or sheets adorned the furniture,
and to step inside
was to step out of line.

Take me back to the days
when children respected their parents,
and their elders…
when they picked their own switches,
appreciated gifts,
and were responsible for chores.

Take me back to the days when
prayer in schools wasn't
against the rules…
when beating your child's tail
wouldn't land you in jail.

Take me back. Take me back
because today there's something we lack.
It's all about crack and cream,
smoking the guy who's on their team.
Or, sporting the new Jordans and Tims,
pushing a phat ride with new rims.
FUBU, leather, and Wu Wear,
cursing at our parents like we don't care.
Skipping school to sell bags of weed,
destroying our bodies by scattering our seed.
Awakening the ancestors who rocked the boat
when we take for granted the right to vote.
Peddling guns that kill our own,
five baby mamas without a good home.
We need to go back.